IDENTIFYING BIAS, PROPAGANDA, AND
MISINFORMATION SURROUNDING

THE BOSTON TEA PARTY

JEREMY MORLOCK

PowerKiDS
press™

NEW YORK

Published in 2019 by The Rosen Publishing Group, Inc.
29 East 21st Street, New York, NY 10010

Editor: Theresa Morlock
Book Design: Rachel Rising

Photo Credits: Cover, Popperfoto/ Popperfoto/Getty Images; Cover, pp. 1, 3, 4, 5, 6, 8, 9, 10, 12, 13, 14, 16, 17, 18, 20, 21, 22, 24, 25, 26, 30, 31, 32 (background) Lyubov_Nazarova/Shutterstock.com; p. 4 f11photo/Shutterstock.com; p. 5 Time Life Pictures/The LIFE Picture Collection/Getty Images; pp. 6, 9, 12, 14, 16, 20, 24, 30 (insert) kontur-vid/ Shutterstock.com; pp. 7, 10, 13 (background) Reinhold Leitner/Shutterstock.com; pp. 7, 8, 13, 15, 27, 29 Courtesy of the Library of Congress; p. 10 https://commons.wikimedia.org/wiki/File:BostonTeaPartyJoyceNotice.jpg; p. 11 https://commons.wikimedia.org/wiki/File:J_S_Copley_-_Paul_Revere.jpg; p. 13 Digital News Library of America; p. 17 Stock Montage/Archive Photos/Getty Images; p. 19 Diego Grandi/Shutterstock.com; p. 21 https://commons. wikimedia.org/wiki/File:Houghton_AC8_Sn612_825h_-_Liberty_Tree.jpg; p. 23 https://commons.wikimedia.org/wiki/Fi le:ThomasHutchinsonByEdwardTruman.jpg; p. 25 GraphicaArtis/Archive Photos/Getty Images.

Cataloging-in-Publication Data

Names: Morlock, Jeremy.
Title: Identifying bias, propaganda, and misinformation surrounding the Boston Tea Party / Jeremy Morlock.
Description: New York : PowerKids Press, 2019. | Series: Project learning through American history | Includes glossary and index.
Identifiers: LCCN ISBN 9781538330654 (pbk.) | ISBN 9781538330630 (library bound) | ISBN 9781538330661 (6 pack)
Subjects: LCSH: Boston Tea Party, Boston, Mass., 1773--Juvenile literature.
Classification: LCC E215.7 M67 2019 | DDC 973.3'115--dc23

Manufactured in the United States of America

CPSIA Compliance Information: Batch #CS18PK For further information contact Rosen Publishing, New York, New York at 1-800-237-9932.

CONTENTS

THE BOSTON TEA PARTY

On December 16, 1773, American **patriots** boarded three ships in Boston Harbor, Massachusetts. They grabbed 342 chests of tea owned by the East India Company and dumped the tea overboard. This event, later known as the Boston Tea Party, was a starting point of the American **Revolution**.

Boston Harbor, Massachusetts

This British print, made after the American Revolutionary War, shows Americans throwing tea overboard. The Americans were careful to destroy only the tea, not other goods. What message did that send?

The importance of the Boston Tea Party was larger than just the waste of tea. The tea itself was valuable, but the act of destroying it was a turning point in the movement toward American independence. To the patriots, the tea stood for England's unfair treatment of the colonies. To the British government and its supporters, the Boston Tea Party was proof that the colonies needed to be tightly controlled.

American colonists and British leaders had different opinions about the Tea Party, government, taxes, and liberty. Their ideas were **influenced** by facts, but also by bias, propaganda, and misinformation.

Bias is a behavior in which one believes that some people or ideas are better than others. It usually results in unfair treatment or judgments. Bias can influence how a person understands and shares information. Propaganda is any idea spread in order to help a cause. It's often false or **exaggerated**. Misinformation is always false. It's often spread on purpose to fool people. In this book, you'll learn to spot bias, propaganda, and misinformation in writing and art from the period leading up to the American Revolution.

Spot the Propaganda

Look at the word choice by the writer of the card on page 7. The writer says the merchants received a commission "to enslave" the nation by selling East India Company tea. This is an exaggerated statement and an example of propaganda. It's meant to influence the reader to feel a certain way about a cause—in this case, to feel angry toward the British East India Company and England itself.

This card from 1773 was addressed to two men planning to sell East India Company tea. Can you spot language meant to sway readers' opinions of the men?

A C A R D.

THE PUBLIC present their Compliments to Messieurs JAMES AND DRINKER.----We are informed that you have this Day received your Commission to enslave your native Country; and, as your frivolous Plea of having received no Advice, relative to the scandalous Part you were to act, in the TEA-SCHEME, can no longer serve your Purpose, nor divert our Attention, WE expect and desire you will immediately inform the PUBLIC, by a Line or two to be left at the COFFEE HOUSE, Whether you will, or will not, renounce all Pretensions to execute that Commission?-----THAT WE MAY GOVERN OUR-SELVES ACCORDINGLY.

Philadelphia, December 2, 1773.

TAXATION WITHOUT REPRESENTATION

In the 1760s, **Parliament** created new taxes to raise money in the American colonies. Many colonists thought this was unfair since they had no representation in the British government. Citizens in England elected members to Parliament, but colonists didn't.

This 19th-century work shows Patrick Henry delivering a speech against the Stamp Act. The artist, Peter Frederick Rothermel, was American. How do you think he's trying to make you feel about Patrick Henry? Why might Rothermel have been biased about this situation?

Parliament passed the Stamp Act in 1765. It added to the cost of all paper products, including newspapers and even playing cards. Colonial governments wrote formal arguments against it to Parliament. Crowds attacked the homes and offices of people hired to sell the stamps. Finally, Parliament repealed, or officially ended, the Stamp Act.

Parliament passed the Townshend Acts in 1767. These laws created taxes called duties on **imported** glass, lead, paper, paint, and tea. In response, colonists refused to buy those items from England. Parliament later lifted most of the taxes, but the duty on tea remained.

Colonial or British Bias?

To most members of Parliament, requiring colonists to pay taxes made sense. They saw the colonies as part of the British Empire. Tax money was needed to pay for the military and government that kept the empire running. But colonists felt cut off from the decision-making process because they weren't represented in Parliament. What could cause members of Parliament and colonists to be biased? How would this influence their decisions?

THE TEA ACT

The British East India Company was a struggling business in the mid-1700s. To help the failing company, Parliament passed the Tea Act in 1773. It removed some taxes the company had been paying to the government and allowed it to sell tea only through its own agents, rather than selling to colonial tea merchants. This hurt the tea merchants' business. This also made the company's tea cheaper, even with the duty on tea from the Townshend Acts. The tea duty remained to make the point that England had the right to tax its colonies.

In response to these events, many colonists **boycotted** tea from England. Some bought tea brought in illegally from other countries. Others refused to drink tea at all.

warning to East India Company tea sellers

Brethren, and Fellow Citizens !

YOU may depend, that thofe odious Mifcreants and deteftable Tools to Miniftry and Governor, the TEA CONSIGNEES, (thofe Traitors to their Country, Butchers, who have done, and are doing every Thing to Murder and deftroy all that fhall ftand in the Way of their private Intereft,) are determined to come and refide again in the Town of Bofton.

I therefore give you this early Notice, that you may hold yourfelves in Readinefs, on the fhorteft Notice, to give them fuch a Reception, as fuch vile Ingrates deferve.   JOYCE, jun.
(Chairman of the Committee for Tarring and Feathering.

☞ If any Perfon fhould be fo hardy as to Tear this down, they may expect my fevereft Refentment.   J. jun.

This 1768 painting of silversmith and patriot Paul Revere shows him holding a silver teapot. How might a tax on tea have affected him as a maker of teapots? Could this create bias?

THE NOXIOUS WEED

Patriots saw the Tea Act as a trick at best, lowering the price of tea but keeping the tax on colonists. And they thought buying the tea would mean admitting that England had a right to tax them.

A Philadelphia writer calling himself Mucius wrote a **broadside** called "To the Freemen of America" in 1773. He stated, "Every American believes, that Parliament have no right to tax America." He told colonists that if they paid any tax on imports, it would give Parliament "a right to strip you of every thing you possess."

Watch the Word Choice

Mucius chose his words carefully and exaggerated several times. Not all Americans agreed with him, but he wrote as if they did. He also referred to tea as a weed to make it sound unpleasant and unwanted. What purpose would these statements and exaggerations serve? Would you call Mucius's statements propaganda or misinformation? Why? How do you think American colonists might have responded to this broadside?

This teapot says "No Stamp Act" on one side and "America, Liberty Restored" on the other. Teapots like this were sold in the colonies after the Stamp Act was repealed. They're a form of propaganda.

Mucius called tea a "**noxious** weed." He said Americans must refuse to purchase it: "This is the measure Americans ought to pursue—this the only means to save your country from destruction."

THE LOYALIST VIEW

Americans who supported England were called Loyalists or Tories. They weren't silent during the fight over the tea tax. A New York Loyalist who called himself Poplicola wrote in a broadside that there was no need for Americans to worry, since no one was being forced to buy tea. "Every Man is left in the full Property of his Money, to give or refuse it as he pleases," he stated.

Poplicola also argued that Parliament had a right to control trade, and the tax was a part of that process. "Their claim over us as British subjects extends as far as the common good requires," he wrote. He explained that England and the colonies were connected like parts of a tree. "Destroy the Parental Trunk and the Branches must perish with it," Poplicola warned.

Primary Source Propaganda?

When searching for clues about bias or propaganda, it's important to look at primary sources. These are writings, objects, art, and other things that were created by people who lived during the time. For example, you must read Poplicola's own words to learn about his opinions. What someone else said about him could be influenced by their own bias and whether or not they agreed with him.

This British print from 1775 makes fun of women in North Carolina who organized a boycott on tea. Who would be the audience for this print? How does it show bias?

15

A WAR OF WORDS

Loyalists accused patriots of misleading the public. Patriots said those who disagreed with them were traitors to the colonies. Loyalist Poplicola said Americans needed to follow Parliament's laws to keep the peace: "Genuine Liberty can only be found in Civil Society . . . without Laws, Civil Society cannot stand."

A patriot writer calling himself "An Old Prophet" in the newspaper *New-York Gazetteer* said people who were helping import tea should be "forced from every place in America, loaded with the most striking badges of disgrace."

Notable Names

Why did writers with strong views on the tea issue use pen names instead of their own? Some might have feared becoming targets for people on the other side. Writers also chose names with special meanings. Mucius and Poplicola were names of ancient Roman heroes. Other broadsides were signed by "A Student of Law," "A Tradesman," and "A Mechanic." How would those names have affected how people viewed their writing?

Samuel Adams was a patriot leader in Boston. He pushed the Massachusetts House of Representatives to oppose Parliament's taxes. Adams helped create the first committee of correspondence, which shared news and organized events among patriots.

He singled out "the **deceitful**, lying, infamous Poplicola." He said Tea Act supporters were "robbers of our Liberty, Property, and Peace."

Would the names writers called each other change the way you thought of people? Why are labels like "liar" and "traitor" powerful?

COLONIAL COMMUNITIES TAKE ACTION

Citizens in Philadelphia, Pennsylvania, gathered in October 1773 and passed a **resolution** labeling the Tea Act "a violent attack upon the liberties of America." They called on the East India Company tea sellers to **resign** and said anyone involved in "unloading, receiving, or vending [selling] the tea . . . is an enemy to his country."

Residents of Plymouth, Massachusetts, passed a similar resolution. However, a few days later, 40 other Plymouth citizens signed a letter warning that the resolution could have "fatal consequences." They said they wished to keep "the blessings of peace and good government" and declared themselves to be "loyal" to the king. How would these resolutions have served as propaganda within their communities?

Colonists sometimes held town meetings where citizens could vote directly on issues. In Boston, meetings about the tea tax were too large for the usual space, so they gathered in the Old South Meeting House.

TENSION IN BOSTON

In early November 1773, Boston patriots sent letters to tea sellers demanding that they reject the expected tea and meet the patriots under the Liberty Tree. The tea sellers refused. They wrote that sending late-night threats was "mean and despicable, and smells of Darkness and Deceit."

The first ship with East India Company tea arrived in Boston in late November. A large group of colonists met and voted to send it back. Massachusetts governor Thomas Hutchinson replied that the meeting was illegal. Patriot guards were sent to watch the ship and make sure no one brought the tea ashore.

Messages with Meaning

Patriots wrote that those who helped with the unloading of the tea would show a "thirst for blood," but it was the patriots themselves who were making threats. Why did they describe the other side as violent? Do you think this is misinformation or propaganda? How would signing the broadsides as "The People" change the way the messages were viewed?

The Liberty Tree in Boston was an important symbol for the patriots. Crowds gathered under the elm tree to oppose the Stamp Act and to hold other meetings. British soldiers chopped down the tree in 1775.

Broadsides around Boston warned that anyone who allowed tea to be unloaded had "an inhuman Thirst for Blood . . . they will be considered and treated as Wretches unworthy to live." These were signed "The People."

THE FINAL MEETING

The law required that imported goods be unloaded and taxes on them paid within 20 days. That deadline was approaching for the first ship, the *Dartmouth*. Two more ships, the *Beaver* and the *Eleanor*, arrived in early December and were guarded by more patriots. The tea sellers wouldn't back down, and the ships couldn't be sent back. Governor Hutchinson had commanded that no ship could leave without a pass.

On December 16, thousands of people gathered in the Old South Meeting House. They demanded that Francis Rotch, the owner of the *Dartmouth*, ask for permission to send his ship back to England. Rotch went to the governor, who again refused. When Rotch returned, patriot leader Samuel Adams told the crowd, "This meeting can do nothing more to save the country."

> Governor Hutchinson was loyal to England, and the East India Company had hired his sons. How would this have influenced his decisions? What biases might he have had?
>
> ⟹

23

THE DESTRUCTION OF THE TEA

The public meeting at the Old South Meeting House ended after the crowd heard Rotch's news. "But, BEHOLD what followed!" reported the *Boston Gazette*, a patriot newspaper. "A number of brave & resolute men, determined to do all in their power to save their country from the ruin which their enemies had plotted, in less than four hours, emptied every chest of tea on board the three ships commanded by the captains Hall, Bruce, and Coffin, amounting to 342 chests, into the sea!! without the least damage done to the ships or any other property.

The Disguise

Reports of the Boston Tea Party referred to those involved as "Indians" or "Mohawks." In fact, the people dumping tea were white colonists, not Native Americans. Mohawk images had been used as symbols of American liberty, though no one knows why. Patriots might have used Native American dress to show that they thought of themselves as Americans and not British citizens. They also wished to hide their identities, since they were destroying property.

"This was the boldest stroke which had yet been struck in America," Governor Hutchinson wrote of the Boston Tea Party. "Their leaders feared no consequences. To engage the people in some desperate measure had long been their plan."

The matters and owners are well pleas'd that their ships are thus clear'd; and the people are almost universally congratulating each other on this happy event."

How does this newspaper article show bias? Why could this story be considered propaganda?

NEWS SPREADS

Patriots in New York, Philadelphia, and Charleston, South Carolina, had already forced the East India Company tea sellers in their cities to resign. They cheered the news from Boston. Citizens in Philadelphia passed a resolution to "highly approve of the conduct and spirit of the people of New-York, Charles-Town, and Boston, and return their hearty thanks to the people of Boston for their resolution in destroying the Tea rather than suffering it to be landed."

In the town of Lexington, Massachusetts, patriots met and "resolved against the use of . . . Tea of all sorts, Dutch or English importation; and to manifest the sincerity of their resolution, they bro't together every ounce contained in the town, and committed it to one common bonfire." What message did these patriots send by burning tea?

This cartoon shows leaders of Parliament and the East India Company plotting with a devil standing behind them. Patriots, dressed as Native Americans, call for "Liberty or Death." How is this image propaganda? What is its message to the viewer?

———————————➤

LOYALIST AND BRITISH RESPONSE

One New York Loyalist wrote, "Now the crime of the Bostonians was a compound of the grossest injury and insult. It was an act of the highest **insolence** towards government . . . it was the destruction of property to a vast amount . . . both a severe and a speedy punishment should be inflicted."

King George III called for action against the colonies, saying, "We must master them or totally leave them to themselves and treat them as aliens." Parliament responded by passing the **Coercive** (or Intolerable) Acts, laws that punished Massachusetts. They closed the port of Boston and replaced local elections with royal appointments. This would only anger the patriots more. Less than two years later, on April 19, 1775, the Battles of Lexington and Concord began the American Revolutionary War.

NORTH

Delaware Bay

From N York

AMERICA

Long Island

THE ATLANTIC OCEAN

From Philadelphia

THAMES. R

I will cram the Tea down the Throate of the New York etc.

I wish we may be able to establish our Monopoly in America

Speak in favour of Liberty. Now is the time to push. Shew your courage

Look at our Monster man act we meet the Spirit upon this occasion, or ause lost. Exuse Ye

We must manage this business with a great deal of Art. Or I see we shall not succeed

and my Sons, and prevent my being Fetterd

We will secure your freedom, or die in the Attempt

I am ready to die with grief and vexation at our Disappointment, do vee vee my hopes of preventing Smill like

Damn the Bostonians, by a great means of the our design.

Th People have discover our design to divide them, we shall never be able to regain their confidence

Tea for America

PLAN for an India Warehouse in America

27